HENRY EKADA

Nulato

HENRY EKADA

Nulato

SPIRIT MOUNTAIN PRESS

ISBN: 0-910871-09-4

Interviewing and Editing:
Yvonne Yarber and Curt Madison

Photography:
Curt Madison (unless otherwise noted)

Material collected September 1979, May 1982 and March 1983 in Nulato, Alaska.

Manuscript approved by Henry Ekada September 1983.

Produced and Funded by:
Yukon-Koyukuk School District of Alaska

Regional School Board:
Luke Titus - Chairman
Donald V. Honea - Vice Chairman
Neil Morris - Secretary
Patrick McCarty - Treasurer
Cheryl DeHart
Eddie Bergman
Patrick Madros

Superintendent: Joe Cooper
Assistant Superintendent: Fred Lau
Project Coordinator: Don Kratzer

Supplemental funding:
Johnson O'Malley Grant - EOOC14202516

**Library of Congress
Cataloging in Publication Data**

Madison, Curt
Yarber, Yvonne
　　Ekada, Henry - Nulato. A Biography
　　YKSD Biography Series
　　ISBN 0-910871-09-4

1. Ekada, Henry 2. Koyukon-Athabaskan
3. Alaska Biography

SPIRIT MOUNTAIN PRESS
P.O. BOX 1214 FAIRBANKS, ALASKA 99707

Cover Photo:
Henry Ekada, 1982.

Frontispiece:
The Ekada family L-R: Sharon, Freda, Henry, Patricia, Evelyn, Judy Madros, Martina holding Brian.

A Note From a Linguist

As you read through this autobiography you will notice a style and a diction you may not have seen before in print. This is because it is an oral storytelling style. This autobiography has been compiled from many hours of taped interviews. As you read you should listen for the sound of the spoken voice. While it has not been possible to show all the rhythms and nuances of the speaker's voice, much of the original style has been kept. If possible you should read aloud and use your knowledge of the way the old people speak to recapture the style of the original.

This autobiography has been written in the original style for three reasons. First, the original style is a kind of dramatic poetry that depends on pacing, succinctness, and semantic indirectness for its narrative impact. The original diction is part and parcel of its message and the editors have kept that diction out of a deep respect for the person represented in this autobiography.

The second reason for keeping the original diction is that it gives a good example of some of the varied richness of the English language. English as it is spoken in many parts of the world and by many different people varies in style and the editors feel that it is important for you as a reader to know, understand and respect the wide resources of this variation in English.

The third reason for writing in the original style is that this style will be familiar to many of you who will read this book. The editors hope that you will enjoy reading something in a style that you may never have seen written before even though you have heard it spoken many times.

Ron Scollon
Alaska Native Language Center
University of Alaska
Fairbanks
1979

Acknowledgements

This book could not be done without generous help from many people. Despite adventures in other parts of the state, Bob Maguire remains the originator of this series. Ron Scollon manages the Gutenberg Dump giving other people linguistic help. Eliza Jones continues to give invaluable advice, translation, and help with the family tree. Madeline Solomon identified many of the people in the Jesuit archive photos during a week at Gonzaga in 1979. Father Bartels, Father Kestler and the Catholic Church's Nulato birth records helped with the family tree. Renee Blahuta spent much time digging out interesting collections from the University of Alaska archives. Bea Hagen typed the transcripts from hours of tape. Janis Carney and Liza Vernet donated their time proof reading. Kris Ann Mountain helped with photo captions. The Nulato school staff put us up and put up with us during our visits, including a Thanksgiving dinner. Joe Cooper, Fred Lau, and Mavis Brown continue to keep things organized at the central office. The Regional School Board of Yukon-Koyukuk School District continue to support local curriculum. And finally at Spirit Mountain Press, Larry Laraby, Doug Miller and Eva Bee march all this material into printed form.

All royalties from the sale of this book go to the Yukon-Koyukuk School District for the production of more autobiographies.

This is the first printing of this book. Please let us know about any corrections for future printings.

Foreword

This book is the seventeenth produced by the Yukon-Koyukuk School District in a series meant to provide cultural understanding of our own area and relevant role models for students. Too often Interior Alaska is ignored in books or mentioned only in conjunction with its mineral resources such as the gold rush or oil pipeline. We are gauged by what we are worth to Outside people. People living in the Interior certainly have been affected by those things but also by missionaries, wage labor, fur prices, celebrations, spring hunts, schools, technology, potlatches, and much more. For residents, Interior Alaska is all of those things people do together, whether in the woods, on the river, in the village or on Two Street. It's a rich and varied culture often glossed over in favor of things more easily written and understood.

This project was begun in 1977 by Bob Maguire. Representatives of Indian Education Parent Committees from each of Yukon-Koyukuk School District's eleven villages met in Fairbanks February of 1978 to choose two people from each village to write about. A variety of selection means were used—from school committees to village council elections. Despite the fact that most of the representatives were women, few women were chosen for the books. As the years passed, more women were added to give a more complete accounting of recent cultural changes.

It is our goal to provide a vehicle for people who live around us so they can describe the events of their lives in their own words. To be singled out as an individual as we have done in this series has not always been comfortable for the biographees, particularly for those who carry the strong Koyukon value of being humble. Talking about oneself has been a conflict overridden by the desire and overwhelming need to give young people some understanding of their own history in a form they have become accustomed to. A growing number of elders who can't read or write themselves think young people won't believe anything unless it's written in a book. This project attempts to give oral knowledge equal time in the schools.

As materials of this kind become more common, methods of gathering and presenting oral history get better. The most important ingredient is trust. After many hours of interview, people often relax to the point of saying some personal things they prefer left unpublished. After editing the tape transcripts we bring the rough draft manuscript back to the biographees to let them add or delete things before it becomes public. Too often those of us living in rural Alaska have been researched *on* or written *about* for an audience far away. This series is meant to bring information full round--from us back to us for our own uses.

Too many people in the Interior have felt ripped-off by journalists and bureaucrats. Hundreds pass through every year, all wanting information and many never to return. Occasionally their finished work may find its way back to the source only to flare emotions when people feel misrepresented. Perhaps a tight deadline or the lack of travel money may be the excuse for not returning for verification or approval. That is no consolation for people who opened up and shared something of themselves and are left feeling betrayed. We work closely with the biographees to check facts and intentions. The books need to be intimate and daring but the last thing we want to do is make someone's life more difficult. We need to share information in a wholesome way. After all, we're all in this together.

Comments about the biographies, their use, corrections, questions, or anything else is welcome.

Curt Madison
Yvonne Yarber
December 10, 1982
Manley Hot Springs
Alaska 99756

Table of Contents

Introduction

Henry Ekada has lived his entire life in the Nulato area. The village is one of the oldest on the Yukon River. It was founded by the Russian creole Malakhov in 1838 as the farthest upriver Russian outpost. Fifty years later the Catholic Church founded its first Alaskan mission at Nulato.

In the days of the sternwheeler riverboats it was not uncommon to see several tied up at the river bank. But as with every village Nulato has changed in the recent years. Nearly everyone has moved out of the old village by the river to new houses above the flood plain. The new community center half way between the two sites is made with modern three-sided logs and plywood.

Henry brings to Nulato a unique blend of three cultures. His father was Japanese, his mother Athabaskan, and his long time job maintaining the largest school of the District makes him an interpreter of Outside technology. It is not easy being different in a village, but Henry has managed to use all of his background to make a fine contribution to Nulato.

Caches in Nulato, 1983.

Glossary

Cat — Caterpillar Tractor Company bulldozer

corduroy — logs laid as a foundation for a road

deadman — an anchor set in the ground; used to tie off a cable

Delo — a brand of motor oil

jimmies — GMC diesel engines

rats — muskrats

roughnecks — oil well drillers

slimers — people who clean fish on the assembly line of salmon processing

sweat pipes — solder together copper pipes and fittings

Local Area

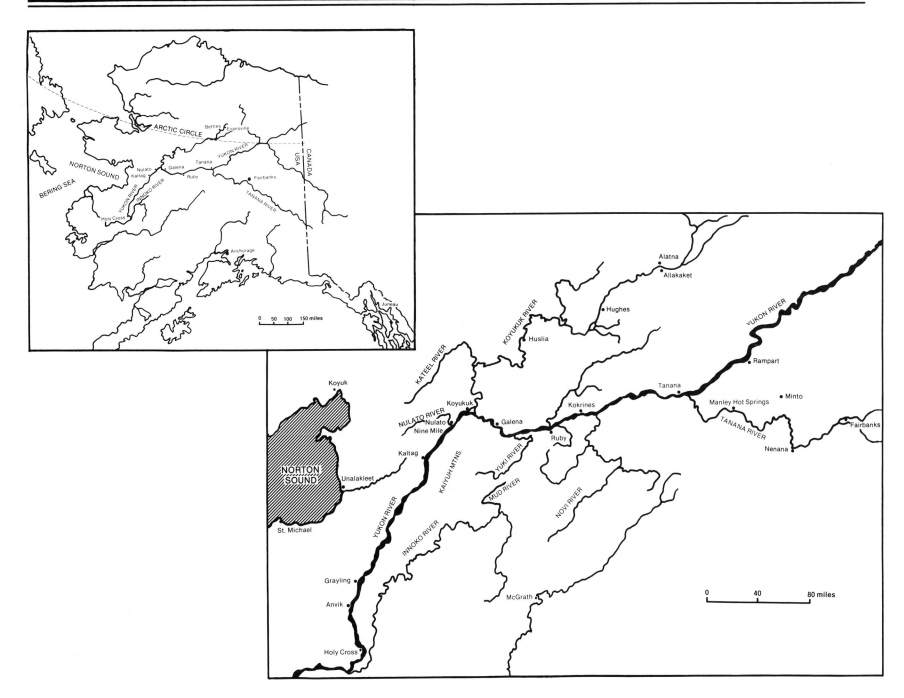

Dad

I was born right here in Nulato, December 21, 1926. Shortest day of the winter. I wasn't eleven years old when my father died of a heart attack right across this Yukon River here.

1937. Springtime. We went out rat hunting. My mother, sister, brother and me. He moved us out in the spring first. My brother came back to Nulato for him and stayed overnight here. Next day going back across the river my father was pulling the sled down with the dogs and he just keeled right over the sled. Heart attack right there. My brother got all excited. He didn't know what to do. This old guy, George Halfway was coming across and he stopped his dogs. He told my brother, "Your daddy died there."

They brought him back to town and next day they came up to get us. It was pretty late in the spring. They buried him for us and we went back out. Flood that spring, we could barely move around and we run out of grub. That's all we had to live on just what

Photo by Jette. Oregon Province Jesuit Archives

L-R: Olga George, Mrs. Olga George Halfway, Charlie Brush in front, and George Halfway who raised Charlie. Nulato, circa 1910.

little grub we had. So we eat fish pretty near every day and rats when we could get them. My mother used to hunt all night and didn't hardly catch any rats. Sometimes they just get four or five. Rats must have been 50 cents or 60 cents a skin that time. Lucky, food was cheap. So we came out after the water went down and sold what little rats we killed. We had to live on that.

This is why I really work, take care of my job. I need the money. Because when I was growing up I desired a lot of kids and my kids got a lot of stuff that I didn't have. I'd think and think when I would get old enough and I start working for myself, I might have as hard time as what my dad had. See. 'Cause there was no aid them days. My mother didn't get any aid. Nothing. But lucky, milk was seven cans for a dollar. Pound of coffee was 50 cents. Them days for a few dollars you can get a little grub anyway. But them days it was really hard for us.

My father wasn't from around here. He was from a foreign country, Japan. He worked his way over here. First he was cook in a restaurant, then in a boat. When he landed here he started trapping. The oldtimers wouldn't tell him how to trap. Yeah, that was a White guy like, they thought. They didn't want to tell him, you see. That was their superstitous, I guess. But he was a Jap, too. He laughed at them after that, he told me. That's why a lot of people call us names while I was being raised.

It really hurt us, too. They bug us a lot of times. Lot of times them guys gave us names and everything. But we still just have to use our head to make a living. You can't do it if you don't use your head.

My dad didn't know how to write in the American way, just Japanese. He didn't have any schooling here, either. But he was a good cook. He used to cook Japanese food for us. That's how we eat a lot of rice right now. People bug us about it a lot of times. Even now they bug my kids about it and they come home feeling bad. That's just the attitude we got and we can't help it. We like it. He used to pick this wild spinach, lamb's quarters from around here. People used to laugh at him. But boy, he used to cook it up and just

13

make a meal out of it. Well, we didn't have no money even when he was living. We didn't have no money or nothing. He was just trying to raise us the cheapest that we can go. We wasn't hungry anyway when he raised us. But after he died like the way I said, there was no aid, no food stamps, nothing. My mother couldn't get no help. Nothing. So we just struggled our way into where we're at now.

My dad used to do a lot of things that the people didn't know. Right up to today. I shouldn't talk about it, but I can tell you a little. We used to fish down here at Nine Mile for kings in the summer. One summer, we were small, he told us, "We got to cut logs. We're going to build a pen house."

We put the walls up about four feet high and pretty soon he cut poles and we nailed them up. Then he had an inboard boat, six or eight horse anyway. We came up to Nulato and got some old sheet iron. He put that on half of the pen roof. The rest was just poles.

Pretty soon he was taking fish upriver that way. Guts and heads. Fish were running yet and pretty soon he started bringing live foxes home. Here he was feeding them foxes all summer with heads and guts. He let them get used to the fish and then he set live traps for them. We stayed year-round down at Nine Mile next to that pen with those live foxes.

As soon as it froze over we set a net under the ice for fish. We have to catch fish for them foxes fresh every day. Pretty soon that pen was just full of fox. Just like you were feeding dogs. Every night you have to go back there and feed them. They get so tame they practically eat right out of your hand.

There must have been twenty foxes in that pen and right up to today them guys didn't know how he caught so many foxes. By Christmastime he started skinning them. He waited until they were just prime. He told us later that was why he left part of the roof open. For snow to go in. They sleep under the tin part on grass, but he gives them fresh snow every day. If it doesn't snow enough, he grabs a shovel and throws it in.

14

My dad was strict with us. We had to work and we had to do what he told us. Even out at camp, ten o'clock was our bedtime. Then if we came into town for Christmas or something, kids running around, dance or anything, we had to be back in at nine o'clock.

We spent one whole winter out at the Innoko. Dad caught a lot of beaver using a net that time. He made the net but I don't know how he did it. Harry Brush, my half-brother, was out with us too. Boy they caught a lot of beaver! But it was cold. Dad packed those beaver no matter how cold.

One time he had two in his pack sack and a string tied across the straps to keep the pack straps off his shoulders. He tied it too tight and that's when he froze his lungs. Breathing that cold air trying to come home packing two beaver. Packing heavy, breathing hard. All that cold air just froze his lungs. I don't think that poor guy could walk out from here to the river bank without stopping, taking a rest after that. He said the pain hit him so bad he just have to stop and rest. But he had to keep going just to make a living for us.

No use going to the hospital. They couldn't do nothing for him. We were at Nine Mile and we could see him coming home from the trapline. You see him coming out of the slough. I don't know how many times, stopping, taking a break, standing to relieve that pain. Then he walks again, stop, walks again, stop. That's how hard he was paining. As soon as he comes home he just lays down the whole evening.

That winter out on the Innoko we were small but I remember it good. We were out playing, sliding down. Pretty soon a plane landed right in front of the camp. I don't know if my father knew he was coming or how he arranged it. The guy came out of the plane and shook hands with my father. We were scared so we ran inside the house. Pretty soon my father brought out all the fur he cached all winter, mink and foxes and sold it. I had one little mink that a mouse ate up. He gave it to me and my mother sewed it up, fixed it for me. Made it look pretty good, but it was small. I got seven

L-R: Authur Ekada, Jimmie Ekada, Annie Ekada, Henry Ekada, Sr., Rita Esmailka

dollars for it. Gee, that was a lot of money. Seven dollars. No place to spend it. We kept that money all winter till we came back out to Nulato.

My half-brother, Harry Brush was staying with us and he took the two dogs over towards Kaltag. Two dogs was all we had. No trail. He was snowshoeing ahead of the dogs all the way to Kaltag. He brought back a sledload of groceries with them two dogs. Whatever little stuff we needed. Good-sized load for those two dogs but he said he didn't have any trouble.

Those two dogs were the only friends we had. Me and my brother. We'd play with them every day. Falltime they were just pups, but by winter they were big because they ate just meat. Them days was hardly any moose over the Innoko but my father killed some and we had it hanging there. And we were eating beaver meat and rabbits. We had a lot of fun and never went hungry for White man grub. We had a lot of that food, I guess, but I didn't know what we had.

Towards spring our father and mother said, "Well, let's slack off on that stuff." Like if we're running low or something. They usually tell us to slack off of it or they quit eating it. Towards end of spring we started getting one slice of bread. They start cutting it for us. Before, we used to help ourself to it. And when our father make cornbread he just let us eat some. We was wondering how come he's doing that? "Well," they said, "We were getting low on food."

School

What little school I had was in the mission school here. We were packed in like sardines. Forty or fifty of us in one room with one nun. At that time my mother was cutting wood for the store and we couldn't even afford to eat lunch at home. So I had to eat lunch at Sister's place. They had a cook and everything there anyway. You get a bowl of soup for lunch and boy you eat just like a...I don't know what. That bowl of soup would mean lots to you.

My mother wasn't home so she didn't cook us lunch. If we do go home, we had to chew dry fish or something. That's about it. She was out checking snares or trying to get something to eat. That's how hard it was.

Nowadays the kids in school eat just like in restaurants. Better than restaurants. Like this winter I went over with the kids to Koyuk. I was surprised the meal they were serving us there. School lunches, but man!

Then I met a guy there that works at the school. He's working there every year because he don't want to lose his job. It was hard for him too when he was getting raised so he got to keep on working. That's the way he tell his kids that, too. Now he says he go up in the school and see them kids eating. Everyday, how good they eat. This guy said the same thing just like the way I said. This young generation think they know everything. They get out of high school go to college for awhile and you can't tell them nothing.

But he said we still know better than them. Now you take them out in the sticks, these kids right here in the young generation, tell them to get poles or something, they wouldn't know what to do. They wouldn't know what poles to get for fish wheel or anything because they don't take interest in it. Long ago if they tell us to get poles, they show us once, then we got to get them kind of poles. Kids nowadays just sit on the bank when all kinds of wood drifting by. They wouldn't try to tow it in for firewood, no. They just want to do it in the wintertime and haul it with sno-go.

We Struggle On

My mother was Annie Ekada. She died in Tanana when she was 83. She was married twice, I guess. For awhile she was married to Bill Burk. That's how Eddie Hildebrand is my half-brother. Same mother but different father. Martha Joe adopted him and he was Esmailka then. She adopted Harold Esmailka at the same time. It was hard them days. But food was cheap. That's how we made it.

Rita, my sister, was raised in Holy Cross so she has a little better schooling than what we had. We had another sister married down there and Rita stayed with her. Our mother couldn't afford to keep us all, I guess. Us, we had to work cutting wood for the store. Lucky them days stores was burning wood, buying wood.

And no snowmachine, we have to feed our dogs. If you got no fish for your dogs you have to buy dry fish. What fish you trade off for groceries in the summer you have to buy back again in the winter to feed your dogs. That's the best friend you had is your dogs. If you didn't have no dogs, nothing, you're just in tough shape.

After my brother went to work, I had to take care of our mother myself. I was fifteen years old. Riverboats were burning wood then. Steamer *Nenana* and Steamer *Alice* going up and down the river burning wood. Old Man Sommers was taking the contract of this wood for the riverboats. He paid seven dollars a cord. You had to haul that wood out, pile it up eight feet high on the bank. I cut sixteen cords of wood before Christmas to make a living that time. That seven dollars a cord was lot of money for us. No chainsaw them days, too. You just have to use one-man saw and you have to worry like hell if you're going to get any grub again. You cannot flash a dollar around or nothing them days. We had no father, no aid, no food stamps. Not like today. Anybody in town got foodstamps. That's what really bugs me. After I start working.

Nowadays kids have good schooling but they don't use it. I'm going to tell you about Harold Esmailka. Harold was just a kid when he got logs with me for fish wheel. We had to borrow my brother's boat. He had an old one-lunger inboard motor. Harold said he was going to go with me. Well, I couldn't hire anybody to help me get logs because I didn't have no money. But this boat of Charlie Brush's was easy on gas. Really easy.

So we went up the river and got five standing logs. Took us all night. Harold was small. After that he went to the mission, Holy Cross Mission.

Holy Cross Mission classroom, circa 1910.

That's where he had all his school. And he said the boys that went to school with him were better mechanic and everything than him. And them boys all they do is just loafing now. Look where Harold Esmailka is. He has his own air service and it keeps getting bigger. That shows what guys that want to use their heads can do.

If I had the schooling these kids had, I would never be around here, too. Nineteen-thirty-seven my father was going to send us out to San Francisco. That's where his sister was. I was going to go to school there. But I think we're lucky that we didn't go because my mother would have been all alone. That would have been hard for her.

We used the logs he helped me get to build that fish wheel and hired somebody to push it down for us. We didn't have no money for a boat or a motor. All we had was a little twelve foot boat. Just like a box. Twelve foot, one-inch-boards, just might as well call it a box. Me and my mother and a little grub. They give us little grub because I was going to trade it off with dry fish, after the fish dry, to the traders. So he gave us a little grub and we went down.

The Hundorf boys, their dad, Max Hundorf, was the Commissioner, were fishing at Four Mile. As I was leaving, they tell me to go use their poles for a fish rack. We need lots of poles to hang all them fish to dry. They said bring the poles down to our camp. But how I'm going to come up there against the current? I have no boat, nothing. Just canoe. I told my mother, "I'm going to go up and get those poles."

"Go ahead," she told me, "How you going to bring them down?"

"I'll tie logs together," I tell her. Couldn't afford to buy even nails that time.

So I paddled up to my fish wheel. It's swift where I got my fish wheel. I drug my canoe around on the beach. I paddled up that night in the canoe. I cut all the stringers on the hill and drug them down. Tie them together with what little rope I had. Then I throw all the poles down on top of the stringers and tow it down in canoe.

We cut lot of fish that summer. I work till twelve o'clock or one o'clock in the morning cutting. I got to bed late. Pretty soon one morning my mother got up. I heard her get up in the morning. She calls me, ''Your fish wheel is floating out up here!''

Here the fish wheel got full and the box is tipped way over lopsided. I had made a deadman, buried it in the ground on the bank, and tied the cable to it. But I didn't bury it deep enough and that wheel dragged the deadman right out. The cable was dragging. But there's big eddy in front of my camp.

Aerial view of Nulato, 1983.

Modern day fish trap on a Nulato cache.

22

That's just what helped me. I jumped in the canoe and paddled out to the wheel. I grabbed the cable and tied what little rope we had to it and tied it into the bank.

Then I get in the little boat and make about three or four trips. I brought all the fish into a little bin we had along the water. We stake logs in a square next to the river and line the bottom with willows. If you lay fish right on the rocks your knife gets dull fast when you're cutting. We change the willows every day. Nowadays we use plastic to line the bin.

I told my mother I'm going to pull the wheel back up. She said okay and got on the wheel so she can hold it out from the beach with a pole. I knock off the paddles so it can move. Just scraping along the beach I pull it up. Well that eddy helped me a lot. But as soon as I hit current I couldn't pull anymore. I had to worry about my mother too. So I tied it up right there and I tell her, "Go ahead. Walk back down to the camp and start cutting fish. I can set it back up."

I didn't know for what. All we had was five dogs. We had enough fish for our dogs already, but because I know I have to sell that fish. I have to trade off for groceries. For the winter, too. I had twelve racks of fish up by the Fourth of July. About 1,000 fish on each rack. Me and my mother. Getting poles and racks up. What worries me, I have to sell fish to get some more groceries, because I have no job.

Cannery Wages

Guys were going to the cannery then and I was thinking about it. I was thinking, thinking right there while I was working on the wheel. Pretty soon Johnny Sommers was coming up. He was running a store in Kaltag. He always stop with me.

I was working at my wheel and he came along again. He stopped and help me set the wheel up and I still got about 700 fish to cut down there. I told him, "Well, Johnny, I'm going to have enough fish for next year fish, too. I'm going to go to the cannery next year, if I could go."

"Oh," he told me, "you're catching a lot of fish. You got that little boat there. Why do you want to go?"

"No," I tell him, "I going to get a boat, engine or something. Inboard or something." He didn't say nothing. He thought I was just talking. After we got through with the wheel I went back down to my mother.

"Mom," I told her, "this is my last year fishing. I'm going to go look for work next summer."

"Tell me. Where you going to go? I don't know if you can go. You drink too much."

And I don't drink that much. I tell her we got no boat. We have to wait for somebody to go by and hope they stop and pick us up. Sometimes they stop. Sometimes they don't. Sometimes we run out of grub. But we don't want to wave anybody in just to go up.

Pretty soon Sommer's wife came down to my mother during fishing. So they had boats and it was a little easier for us then because we had a way to bring up our fish. I filled up what little cache I had and sold fish for seven cents a pound for sun-dried fish. Seven cents a pound that time, but you could get lot of groceries for couple dollars.

That really fixed me up. I had plenty of fish so next summer I went to the cannery, 1945. Boys was working over there. I stayed near two months in Bristol Bay. I made 700 dollars. Lot of money that 700 dollars. So I ask Sommers' boy, Johnny Sommers had a mill down in Kaltag, if he had boat lumber. "Can I buy it?" I ask him. He even brought it up for me. And his dad had little air-cooled seven horse motors. Inboard motors.

Right there I bought this stuff with the 700 dollars. I bought all the material and the engine. Already I had a nine horse Johnson outboard that I bought for 250 dollars, but I didn't have money to get the boat built. Then

Eddie Hildebrand said he'd build it if I gave him the kicker. I was glad. I had a boat with an inboard motor.

That fall we went over to Mud River with Eddie Hildebrand, my mother and me. I was still single. My mother made out a list for the trader of the stuff we was going to get. He added it up and it was 400 dollars. That's for the whole winter. But that was too much for him. "Gee, that's quite a bit of grub," he said. He knew I had to trap to pay that off but he can't depend on me. I was pretty small yet.

"Well," my mother said, "that's all right. We'll make it." she scratched off a lot of stuff.

We stopped in Kaltag on the way over. Johnny Sommers had a store there. We didn't want to get too much credit there either, but we got a little more stuff. We stayed out the whole winter till after beaver season. We paid off that 400 dollars and then we had a little more money to spend. I wouldn't say how many beaver I caught because there was a limit in those days. And there still is today. But I caught a pretty good number of beaver. Enough that we could live on it all summer without getting hungry. We couldn't live classy, but we could live on it. We lived pretty good through that summer all on account of we didn't have to be shy to get anything in the store because we had the money to get it. Don't flash it around though, we just get what we need and that's it.

Chapter Two: Working At The Oil Camp

Learn About Tools

I took a load of fish up to town from camp. Summer 1959. My mother was down there alone and a chopper landed. Next day they came back. They start talking to me, "Can we level out this place? Can we make a dock here?"

"What you guys going to do?" I ask them.

"We're going to drill for oil. We're going to make a base camp right here."

But that hill was steep right into the river. I told them to go ahead if they promise me a job. He said he'd pay for it and everything and not bother our camp. I told them to go ahead and they took off. I thought they were going to come in right away. We moved everything. A lot later a barge came down with some stuff.

People start coming down looking for some jobs, but these guys promise me they would hire me first. So I just stayed in town and waited. Pretty soon a chopper came and they told Charlie Brush, my half-brother, and me to go down and sign in if we wanted to work. We went down but we couldn't stay in camp. We had to run back and forth from here. They built fourteen miles of road and had us cutting corduroy to put under all that stuff they unloaded from their big boats. Then they laid us off again until they finished their road.

I thought they were through with us for good. Man, then I started worrying again. I was married already with a bunch of kids. Pretty soon they came back and got us on again. They tell us we're going to stay in camp now. Next morning we went out by helicopter back fourteen miles there. Just like a little place there. They had everything all straightened out. No camp though, just Quonset hut was up.

This foreman told me to start the oil stove. I didn't even know how fire-pot oil stove start. He fooled around with it. He didn't know how to start it, either. I just stayed right on top with him. I was just watching what he was doing. Pretty soon we seen oil coming in so we throw match in there and it lit. Next one was easier.

Then the mechanic came and carpenters. They built thirteen bunkhouses and a mess hall. They put each of the cabins up in one day. "You and Charlie are going to take care of camp," they tell me. Charlie was my half-brother but he gets mad, too. I know he wants to come home. He starts getting mad at me. Well, he'd had experience couple years before that. But me, my first time at an oil camp. I didn't even know how to drive a Cat. Didn't know nothing. Well, Charlie was really getting cranky. I know he was getting cranky to this mechanic that's going to stay at the camp and take care of the equipment. But I was lucky I had good guys to work with.

The foreman from the derrick came to me and said "Lets get on that D-6 fork lift and haul a barrel of Delo for the drilling rig up there. Later on the roughnecks are going to run out of oil up there and nobody's going to know how to drive a Cat. You better learn."

I watch this mechanic how he drive this Cat. Follow him around when he gets on the Cat or any kind of equipment. Pretty soon I get on. Well I didn't know quite how to deal with it, but I keep looking at it. So I got it walking. It was about a quarter of a mile to where that oil and gas was piled. The first barrel I came to I punched my forks through the barrel. Boy, I got scared. Well hell, I thought I was going down the road. Get fired.

"We got to learn," the boss said. "It just takes time to learn." Lucky that whole outfit didn't mind about their equipment. So we lift the forks up again, try the next one.

27

"Can we roll it on the forks?" I ask him.

"No," he said, " we're not supposed to lift over fifty pounds. That's what the machine is for."

But hell, I lift over 150 pounds, that's all I know. That's how I work, I told him.

"We're not going to lift it, just roll it." "Okay, let's try it," he said.

We rolled it. Got it on the forks. Then I started sweating again. I didn't know how to get out of there. We were squeezed in tight. Well, the guy said we had to learn. Nobody around us. Somehow I scraped this one barrel of gas. The tracks scraped and made a little hole in it. But he said it was nothing we had to learn and I was proud.

Then I start sweating again. We walked it up to the derrick and I know I got to squeeze in again. These guys that operate Cats, it's nothing to them. When we got up there all I know was, I'm just going to lift it some way. Do it the hard way.

We got there and I ask him how we're going to do it. He just try to get me to squeeze in again, but he don't know how to drive a Cat either. I just dropped it right there, put it down. I said to hell with it, I'm going to roll it. That's only the way I know how to work. Do it the hard way. He just walked away from me. "Go ahead. Use your own judgement," he said.

I had to lift it up on barrel racks. So I laid planks against it. Pretty soon these roughnecks stop working and they look at me. "Boy, you Indians work hard," they said.

"That's just the way I was raised, working hard," I tell them. "I never had it like this, easy. I have to work hard." That got me kind of mad, you know. Then I didn't say anything. I didn't know how to do it, but I got the barrel there anyway.

Pretty soon the superintendent came out to me, called me by name. He told me, "You got nothing to do with that derrick up there. Nothing. Your job is supposed to be taking care of the light plant and fueling up the camp.

That's all your job. Who told you to haul that barrel of fuel?"

I thought he saw the barrel up there where I punched a hole through. I thought here I am going down the road. I was sweating. "Don't ever fool around up there with them guys' stuff. If they're running out of anything, let them get it. And if they ask you to do something again you tell them no, it's not your job. If they get mad at you or they tell you something, tell them to come visit me."

Thirteen bunk houses was all there was to do, but Charlie, he hides from us. He gets mad at us. When this guy tells us to learn to drive that Cat around. Gee, that was my glory. Jesus fright, there was my chance to learn something. I was learning a lot of things what I didn't even know the names of. Lot of different names. Lot of guys working there had schooling and everything and they didn't know. But me, I don't know because I don't know. I had to ask the guy, "What's the meaning of that? What that means?" The guy is glad when you ask something like that when you don't know. That's why I keep asking. That's the way to learn. Some guys, you ask them for something but they don't know what it means. The guy has to go over and get it himself. It's right in front of them but they don't know what it means. I had to ask and ask. Maybe sometimes them guys got tired of me. But they were glad of what I was asking. I was asking because it was first time I was working for that kind of a job.

Gee, I thought I was great driving that Cat. Later on the Cat started breaking down and the mechanic tell me, "You better come into the shop and start taking Cats apart with me. You want to?"

"That's the best thing I ever heard," I tell him.

He was sitting on his bench and he told me to just take something off the easiest way I could. I was glad. I start taking them apart. Sometimes I don't even know how to turn the bolts. But I was lucky that guy was old and he was easy going guy. He tell me I'm turning the wrong way. Then he gave me a rachet. I didn't even know how to adjust that rachet. I didn't know about tools. My father didn't have no tools or nothing. We couldn't afford to have tools. But this oil camp had tools up to your neck. I was surprised to see all of them. I didn't even know that tools was like that. All I know was 8-inch cresent wrench and 6-inch. That's all I know. I didn't even know what socket looked like. Gee, I was surprised.

When we started he told me give him half-inch drive. Well, I'm stuck right there. I didn't know what he meant. So I just stand there. He have to come down and show it to me. And he tell me this is 3/8 drive right here. Two different size that's all we got. Numbers is on the socket he tell me. Then he show me the numbers. It was real good. It was easy then. Jesus fright, I learned lots in that oil camp.

Welding

Later that winter he tell me, "You want to learn to weld?"

I tell him, "Sure, that's the best thing you ever tell me." I picked up all the scrap iron around the shop. I brought it over to the welder. "Go ahead and start up the welder." I tell him, "Okay." I start the welder, but no arc.

"What's the matter?"

I tell him. "No arc."

"You got something wrong. You got to think for yourself now." I was stuck right there. "You know what's the matter?" I don't say nothing. He call me. "You know what's the matter? You don't have it grounded."

Well, I don't know. "I didn't know that," I tell him. "First time I'm fooling around with it." But he tell me looks like I really want to learn it. I tell him yeah. His name was Jimmy Stoddard.

"Clamp it. Anything you're going to weld, clamp it to the iron. Ground it."

Pretty soon I got arc. He told me to put on a helmet. Well I seen him using a helmet so I knew what it meant then. I started fooling around. It get stuck with me and everything, you know. Then he'd stop me and tell me how far to pull it away from this iron to weld. Oh, it was the glories that time. I thought I was in glory. I thought I can weld anything. I burned up maybe fifty pounds of rod that day. Long days in March, nothing to do, I went right back there welding. Right after lunch, right after dinner, I burned up another half a can of welding rods. Gee, I thought to myself, I'm gonna start making stuff.

I went back over to the bunkhouse. We were sleeping in one bunkhouse, me and him because we were on alert twenty-four hours a day taking care of the camp. I told him I weld all this time. "Okay," he tell me, "How easy was it?"

"Pretty easy," I tell him.

"Yeah, good that's easy. Tomorrow you're going to try something different. You ever tried overhead welding?"

"Well," I tell him. He got me stuck again. Overhead welding. I didn't know what overhead welding means. "No," I tell him, "I know how to weld now a little bit anyway."

"Tomorrow morning after we get through checking everything out, after coffee break, we'll try it."

"Six o'clock we go to work in the morning taking care of the light plant. That's where I started my maintenance, taking care of the plant. Check the gauges, check the fuel, check the oil. He was working in the shop. I still was thinking of this overhead welding. I didn't know what he meant. He got through with what he was doing. Right away I done what I supposed to have done. I'm still thinking of this welding. What is it? I kept looking at my time. I thought to myself when the heck is going to be coffee time? Ten o'clock is coffee break. I drink up coffee right away and went back down again. I start picking up scrap iron again and started welding again. It was just my glory. This welding what I was doing it looked really good to me.

Nice. Just fine. Gee, I thought I'll get a job any place welding. Next he tell me, "You chip your flux off?"

When he said flux, I don't know what that means, too. I thought we're not even supposed to hammer our bead. "Get your chipping hammer." Well that's where I got stuck again. Chipping hammer. I don't know what means chipping hammer. Then he goes to the tools with me.

"This is what they call chipping hammer. And the flux you have to chip off your welding. Take your welding. It looks good but all that flux is on it yet." He hit, chipped this welding. Well, that welding, Jesus fright, look like hell. Gee, I got embarrassed.

"That's okay,," he tell me. "You'll learn. Now remember, just keep trying. Go so far, get your chipping hammer and chip it. You'll see the mistakes that you're making. You'll see if you go too fast or you go too slow or you got it too high or too low. And you gonna watch how it's flowing."

Well, I don't understand all what he's meaning so I stopped right there. He made couple beads like that. He's a good welder and mechanic and everything, but he made a bum weld to show me. I keep bugging him about how fast to go and how high and everything. Then he done a good finishing welding right in front on top the iron there. I was really watching him. He had to let me use the helmet. I kept trying, trying, trying. Now I can weld and braze from learning that. Just from the oil camp that I was working with. But I was lucky I had a good mechanic that showed me all what little I know. Now I can sweat pipes or anything.

My brother Arthur in Tanana was the same way when he got a job there. He was interested in what another guy was doing. That's just the way we were. We had to be like that because we didn't have no schooling.

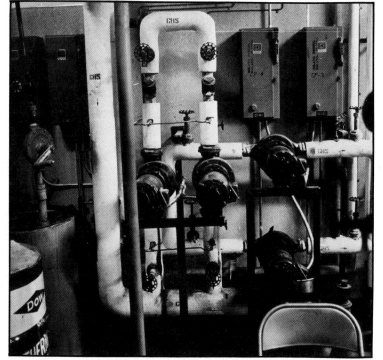
Nulato school boiler room maintained by Henry.

Same way when Northwest was building this school here. They told me I would have a lot of instruments to run this school. Every job they have they bring in a special man for it from Outside. I have to follow that guy around. Even I was off work and not getting paid, because I had to run this place just by myself. I want to learn more about what they are doing. I follow around the boiler man. I follow around the plumbers. I asked them how much heat to work copper and a lot of different things that I don't know yet. Now I got it all in my head. Lot of guys come to us for brazing or anything., I can weld, braze, gas braze, all what I learned.

Lot of guys from here went up on the North Slope. I could have worked there when they first started. Guys come down here and tell me to fill out application. But I don't want to go. They tell me fast money up there, really fast. Tell me fill out this application you can get up there right away because I have the experience of the drilling rigs. I told them no I got a year around job. After the North Slope is done, I'll have no job. Somebody else will have my job at the school. They tell me nothing but big money, but I think I can make just as much in the long run working at this school here. After the pipeline is done, it's done. But the school will be still going.

Clean Up Camp

Well at that oil camp they drilled down 3015 feet without oil. A dry hole. That's all the money would allow them to go. Just enough for one hole. I asked the geologist what they're drilling for and all. I used to visit him every day. I wanted to learn more about this oil drilling. He got all the samples as it comes up. The rocks just float up and get screened.

He tells me what they got each foot. He's got magnifying glasses to watch them rocks. He let me look. You could see all the different colors. Then they lost a gear tooth down at the bottom. Three inch diameter gear tooth. They had fifteen feet more to drill. Fifteen feet more before they were going to cap it off. They said they lost a drill. I hear them coming out of the hole. You hear them twelve Jimmies just humming when they're coming out of the hole. They said it would take three weeks to drill the last fifteen feet if nothing went wrong. But they lost the gear tooth. Boy I thought to myself, this is where the fun is going to start. I don't know how the hell they'll get it out 3000 feet down. The inspector was right there, too. But they got that bugger out. They just sent something down and had it right out. It was surprising.

And they had some kind of instruments outside of the derrick big as this room. A whole panel of instruments. They sent something down there to take pictures of the hole. I asked the guy running it what's all them instruments for. Well they tell me the instruments doing that, this one doing this, all of them doing what they're supposed to be doing. Pretty soon a red light comes on. He said, "The wire is down at the end of the hole now. I'm going to start taking pictures." All the instruments start jumping forth and back when he pressed a button. It was all going on tape. I don't know what kind of tape but he said if they had a machine to play it he would show me how it works. He had to take it back Outside to run it through.

Then they had to cap off the hole. They have to pour cement down seventy-five feet in the pipe. They said there might be gas or oil down there and it might explode so they cover it up with a seventy-five foot plug of cement.

Then they told us to clean up the camp. We made a pit with a Cat. And we drag about twelve foot long by twelve inch thick iron around. We just barely handle it with the Cat. Cannot lift it, just drag it around. We drag that whole place. When we passed inspection the ground was like when we first moved in. If we find a cigarette butt where we were dragging it would never pass inspection. We were doing that for one whole week. When they cover the hole back up we have to level it off. Not even a piece of paper or a piece of can could be sticking up. Not even a drum.

Chapter 3: Trapping and Fishing

On The Kaiyuh Trail

I was watchman over at the oil camp until 1963 but I wanted to go trapping during that time, too. I kept bugging Kentucky to go trapping with him, beaver trapping. He was getting old and ready to go any time he thought, but he had a good trapping area up there.

Finally he made up his mind and told me to go ahead go with him. Nineteen-sixty-one I went with him for beaver. "We'll have two tents," he told me. "I'll show you the country around the last tent and you can trap around there later."

We went to his first tent and stayed there three or four days putting out sets. Then we went up towards Kaiyuh Flats. We were going, going, going. Hardly any snow that year. You can lead your dogs right through any place. I didn't know the country, me, so I had to wait for him. He caught up and said, "Go right across the lake and you'll find a portage there. See that spruce tree up there? We'll head for that one. There is trail right there." I was getting tired, dogs was getting tired, but I started snowshoeing ahead.

We made camp and next day he said we're going to walk around. Just like open country around there. He told me, "When you get on the hump, you look for birch patch, birch humps, you know. That's where the lakes are around there."

I said okay and took off. I got on one hump. Pretty soon I see a birch patch right ahead of me. Sure enough there was a lake there. I went to this birch patch and here was a beaver chewing. Fresh chewing. So I know there is a beaver house in there. I went out on the lake and found the house way over there. Went up to it and it was alive. I put in one side-set. I know he's going to put in sets there, too.

I found four houses in that day and came back to the tent. He was there. He said he put in two sets and there's more. Then I tell him just about where I went. He said, "Tomorrow we're going to make a circle in all that country. I'm going to break trail."

Gee that guy, I don't know how he remember all that country anyway. I had come back the same way I went because I didn't want to get lost. Pretty soon he tell me, "Your trail should be in that lake. You went to the first patch?"

"I don't know," I tell him. I couldn't remember. "Everything look the same for me."

"Well you should have gone to that first patch. I think that's the way you went." I had told him what kind of lake. I kind of picture the lake how it went. "It's right over there. We'll go there, hit that lake, and make short cut to the tent because it's getting late."

I said okay, but I thought, no way. I was walking ahead of him. I thought to myself, hell we're gonna be way the hell off the tent. Then, son-of-a-gun, coming into a birch patch I didn't know where I was, here was where I had knocked down a birch for beaver bait. How did that guy remember?

Jimminy Christmas! Sure enough he made short cut all right. Didn't take us very long to get to the tent. Here I made a big bend for nothing. The next year he told me to go ahead and trap around where I trapped the year before. So I went there by myself and trapped for I don't know how many years.

Kentucky, Lawrence Saunders, was his name. That guy used to catch a lot of fur. Now that country is just around there for nothing. He didn't have no kids. Nice trapping area. Fred Sommers traps part of it now and he's doing good with marten and beaver. He's got a snowmachine. Our days we used just dogs. We struggle with our dogs but we never break down. Sure to come home.

A couple weeks ago I went up the Kaiyuh again. John Sommers was springing out and he said the geese came in, few came already. Eddie and I planned it to go out on the weekend. People going up and down during the week and tell us there's lot of geese. I left ahead of Eddie because he was taking care of the mail plane. He had a high powered snow machine anyway and I had only a little Elan. I told him I'll wait at a certain lake.

Long ago that was the spot that my brother Arthur left me. We stayed under this spruce tree, cold and miserable. Deep snow, breaking trail ahead of the dogs, we were trying to go to Kaiyuh. Sitting there he told me, "Henry, this is my last year on this trail. I'm going to go look for work. And you," he said, "you'll still be on this trail beause you drink."

I didn't said nothing. Miserable. We're just siwashing it out. Next day we made it to Kaiyuh, stayed a couple days and came back. So this spring I was going there with snow machine. Sitting on the snow machine just riding. When I seen this one spruce tree again I thought of my brother. How easy it was right now compared to them days when we was using dogs. Good crust to go on. You could just drive anyplace. Pretty good right now. Now things is so easy. All you got to have is just your gas and oil.

Then I got to this lake where I said I'd wait for Eddie. I just got there and started fooling around and here he comes. He knows more about the Kaiyuh than I do. When we got to John Sommer's camp we had lunch. "Which way we're going to go?" he ask me.

"I just have to follow you," I told him back.

He took off towards where they see all the geese. But what happened, it got so cold where the water was rushing down it just froze up again. They just run across it with snowmachines. There was a bunch of guys up there already getting them geese. Eddie said wait here at one creek while he went up and try to chase geese down to me.

We got to this lake where a guy was going to start a store one time. Store Cabin they call it. Nobody lives there now. Eddie took off and I waited, but all I see was about six geese flying a mile high.

He came back and asked if I saw anything. "No," I tell him, "just six flying about a mile high." That's the ones he said he chased off up there. So I asked, "What we're going to do?"

"Well let's go back and look down this way." He had a high powered snow machine but he didn't want to run away from me. He just take it way ahead and I keep right on his tail. I had this little Elan just going. John Sommers was at his cabin. We asked him. "What you got? Any ducks?" He said no geese. It was too cold.

We started back down about midnight and boy you could just see your breath coming down the trial. Must have been five below. Cold for early part of May. Then I look at that tree again. I know it well. Snow was crusty. When you go on the crust with snow machine it's just like this table, you can go anywhere. I kind of cut into the little bank towards that tree. I want to take a good look at it again. I thought of my brother. That's where my brother said it to me and I'm still on this trail. He's retired out in Arizona now.

Fishing Commercial

I started out fishing with my half-brother Eddie Hildebrand. That's where I learned to make a wheel. But I thought to myself we cannot stay with somebody else every year. We just have to do it ourself. So I moved down to Six Mile. There was a fish camp there before me. Some old guys fished there but they died and nobody wanted that place anymore. Ever since then I been fishing there and now I got an allotment there.

We got a commercial license in 1974 but it was a really poor year. All we sold was just a few pounds of eggs. Nineteen-seventy-five we just sold egg roe, too. Finally 1976 is when everybody hit it. Guy named Staniford bought fish for 85 cents a fish. Then we had to rent a truck for ten dollars a trip to haul it up to the airport. Us, the fishermen, had to get that truck. He just didn't go at it right. Nothing. He had those kids working up there all night. But he made money flying it out of here.

Summer 1979, I had it rough. The biggest bit of fish we got around here is the Fourth of July just about. That's when the fish hits heavy. And that's when my son drowned. We put our wheels into the beach and searched around there. And then, well, I couldn't fish. We were searching for thirteen days. All them guys were all fishing. They were all fishing while we were searching. We lost a big year there.

These days young guys no matter how much education they get they just can't know what to do. Like last spring, I hired some boys. Just got through with twelfth grade. Got out of school with all the education he needed. I brought him down to help me set the wheel. He don't know what to do. I had to keep hollering at him what to do so I brought him back up. I thought no use to have him on the wheel. He might fall in. My wife and I went back down. She been helping me since 1974 when commercial started. She can push out the wheel by herself while I'm standing on it. We don't even use pry.

When I first started I used to pry like hell. But it's so swift you couldn't even hardly budge that wheel. I told my wife some way it should be easier than this. I pull the pry pole down and still I can't budge the wheel. My wife try to push the rocks behind the spars. Nothing. Too heavy. I tell her, "No. this is too much like work. I got something at home that will do the work for us. What I got that come-along at the house doing? That should be right here."

"How you're going to do that?" she said.

"We'll just get back in the boat, go up and get it. I'll fix it to where you'll just use your one hand to push this wheel out."

"No way that you could hook it up." she said.

"Okay," I tell her, "just get in the boat and let's go." Our wheel was still standing straight up. Couldn't hire nobody. We came up and ate dinner. We're still talking about that wheel. She's telling me, ''Get somebody to help you push it out.''

''You're going to push that wheel out by yourself while I'm on it. I got everything fixed up.'' She got kind of mad.

''No. No way that I'm going to push that wheel by myself. If you can't push it, I don't see how I'm going to push it.''

I got a sledge hammer and an inch and a quarter pipe about three feet long. We went back down. I drove that pipe in the beach right at the water line. Then I tied a rope back to the end of the spar log and hooked the come-along to it. I tell her, ''Here, go ahead, push it out and I'll go out and measure the water.'' She look at me.

''Gee, you're crazy. How in the hell you think I'm going to push it out?''

''Just crank that come-along with one hand. Push it out. It's like Samson,'' I tell her, making fun. She got mad at me again.

''Go ahead,'' she tell me, ''start the wheel. Try to start it. Show me how you're going to do it.''

I said okay and grabbed the handle of the come-along and start cranking. Pretty soon the wheel started going. I told her to try it. She grabbed it and started cranking. Pretty soon the wheel got deep enough to where it'll turn. ''See,'' I told her. ''You're just like Samson. See how easy it is''

From there on we used that come-along. I tell lot of people and still a lot of them didn't understand how I hook it up. So I tell them you just have to think. When you're working hard by yourself you should think. Guy have to stop to think how things can go easy.

Now this summer, 1982, the way the rumors go I don't think they'll be buying fish. Just the roe. Now we got to cut every fish that we're pulling the roe out of. That's going to be back like when we used to do it for a living. Like cutting fish for our dogs. When we get a fish in our wheel we cannot reject it. We have to cut every one of them and hang them up. That's going to be a lot of work again this summer just like the old days doing it for our dogs.

We cut two different ways for people and dogs. Ones we cut for dogs we don't wash. We just cut it and throw it on the ground and let somebody keep hanging them up on racks in the sun and rain. But eating-fish, what we call eating-fish, we got to take good care of it, put it out of the rain and smoke it. Sun kind of cooks it so we keep it away from the sun. Put it in the smoke house and make sure flies don't get to it. Everything like that.

I get off work the first of July for two weeks during the king run. We got to get up about four o'clock to go down to the net. We come back, unload

Boats on the Yukon river bank at Nulato.

the fish, haul it up to where my wife is going to cut it then I take off again. Back down to the wheel to start hauling fish. Last year the season was only three days each week so we have to run twenty-four hours.

Last year, too, they reject a lot of fish back to us. The inspector from Seattle was right there on the bank where they're buying fish. Pink fish and red meat was all they'd take. You have to stay at the dock for maybe a couple hours. By then the fish cutters are nearly through so we have to bring another boatload of females to them to pull the roe out. If they do it that way again this year, we'll only go after the king run. My boy is working so I got no help now. I'll try to get some kids to help me to run the wheel.

Sidney Huntington was buying roe here for $2.25 a pound. Then about the middle of the season Sweetsir came down and offered $3.50 a pound. Sidney had to raise his price to meet the other one's so he could get some eggs. That was pretty good. And it made the females valuable.

So what we were doing, we kept somebody out on the wheel all the time. We had a two-by-eight and a chute on the box of the wheel. We watch. If the wheel scoops up a male we lift the board and let him scoot back into the river.

It works good but you really get tired watching that wheel. I tried my kid doing it but I worried more about him than what I was trying to do. If I stay there myself I don't worry about them. If anything happened, I got the boat and everything ready. But I got to haul loads up to town and then they got no boat. They might fall asleep and fall in the river. So boring waiting for a fish to come up in the dip. The Game Commissioner saw our setup and said it was alright. It just scoops the fish right back into the river. Doesn't hurt the fish or nothing.

All those eggs go right to Japan. Japanese guys stay in the processor in Galena curing them right there. I never seen the plant operating but I guess Huntington has a hard time keeping the crew going. They have to go around the clock as long as the fish are coming in. They're hauling fish up there steady. The slimers have to keep going as long as we're going us, too. They have to go around the clock to keep up with us. He has to pay them good.

Last summer we were all getting tired. Girls and everybody getting tired down there. I came up with a load of fish and I saw one guy walking the street. "Hey, Percy!" I call him. "Can I hire you. Pay you same price as what these guys are getting." He say sure. "Get your...you don't have to take nothing. We got everything down there. I'll board you and everything. Just take your coat or raingear or whatever you got." He said he'd put on old clothes.

"And I'll go twenty-four hours," he said.

Boy he make me happy when he said he's going to go twenty-four hours. So he started, but by midnight that night he was just curled up on the rocks back there. I asked him what happened. Oh, he said he got tired. He just went to lay down and went to sleep right there. We had a lunch and I said, "I thought you said you was going to go twenty-four hours?"

"Oh," he said, "it's too hard."

I was paying ten bucks an hour and he didn't quite make a week. Fishing was three days a week season, but he put in quite a few hours. I told him to come around to pick up his pay anytime. His check was already made out in the house. He never did come around for a long time. I was glad. I thought he was saving it. Finally one day he came in and tell me, "I need a little money."

"Look how much you made in three days," I told him. "If you had stuck it out with me look, you would have doubled that thing. If I was in your shoe when I was getting raised up as young as you, I would go the twenty-four. I would never think about sleeping. I would be thinking of making that money. When I was your age, if I make that much money I don't know what I would do with it."

And he just smiled and walked out. "Yeah."

Chapter Four: Working School Maintenance and My Son

Henry Ekada at work in Nulato school.

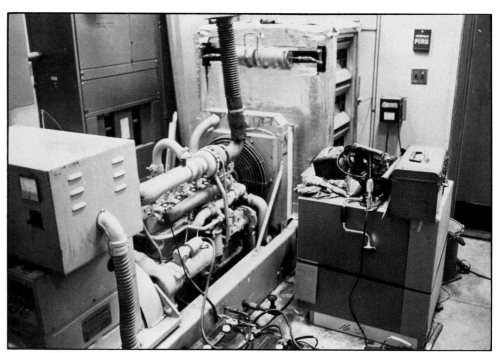

Equipment Henry keeps going at the Nulato school.

Figure Out Why It Works

You know all these years I never get overtime for working at this school. I work seven days a week in the wintertime at fifty or sixty below. I put in whole days on the weekend and I never get no overtime for it. I know that if something is going to go wrong I have to be right on top of it. If I let it go, it will be that much more work for me. On a construction job if you work overtime you get paid for it. But here if there's something wrong I have to fix it, seven and a half hours on the job or not. I have to do it myself.

Like last winter a furnace bearing went out. Just nothing left of it. I got on the phone to order a three-quarter-inch bearing. You think I got it? No way. The parts finally came in last week about six months later. I just started thinking. Lot of stuff when you're alone you have to think about it. So I put in a sno-go bearing. That bearing lasted right up till last week. Seems like you always got to know *why* something works not just *if* it works.

Last fall they called me from Koyukuk to say their boiler went out. They didn't have enough glycol in their lines and one froze and burst. I couldn't figure it out right away. I started up the boiler. The water gauge ran up to thirty degrees and it kicks off. It's set to run up to one-hundred-sixty degrees and here it get to thirty degrees and trips off! Jimminy Christmas I thought, no water. I spent the night there in the light plant house thinking about it. I ask Roger, the maintenance man there and he doesn't know.

I came to a check valve on a half inch pipe. Gol darn it! This is man-made I thought to myself. Man put it up. I can work on it, too. I got kind of pissed-off. I took the check valve off and there's supposed to be raw water. Supposed to automatically fill the boiler when it runs low. No water. Right there I told this guy the line is froze.

"Well, let's tear up the utilidor," I tell him. We hired a guy and shovel off all the way. We even put up lights so we could work in the dark. When we tore the lid off, sure enough eighty feet of that pipe was busted. All froze

45

and cracked. "Who put these pipes in?" I asked him.

"Those guys that put the boilers in."

"They put any heat tapes on it?"

"I don't think so."

So I went under the building and cut this line off right away. Roger asks me if I ever did that before. I told him I'm going to tear out all the pipes. Just like he didn't believe me. "I know what I'm doing, Roger," I tell him. I can fix it. If I had the pipes here I would fix it today."

Henry standing by a truck filled with goods going to his brother Eddie Hildebrande's store.

I called in to Nenana and told them the pipe broke and no heat tapes on it. Then I came back down to Nulato, got some pipes and went back up. Not enough anti-freeze in the boiler lines. I brought my tester up and told Roger we'd register it for fifty or sixty below. We have to keep that water circulating. That's what is heating the buildings.

He said the pipes were making a lot of noise, too, like they were going to bust before the boiler quit. That's because it was lacking water. Pipes heat up too fast when that line froze and that steam was popping the pipes. They got thermostats on the pipes and they're going to call for a certain temperature. But that raw water was froze up and water is not flowing steady. It was just pushing steam. Finally he see the point. And then I broke my tester. Since then I been calling for a glycol tester and still never got it yet.

No matter what though I'm going to push through here till I retire. Just the way my brother did. Another fourteen years and I think I'll have it made. Long years. Then I'll just take it easy. Maybe travel around the country or look at the world. I'd like to go down around Japan to see the country my father was from. I heard that it's pretty good looking. Simeon Mountain went down with some school kids and I heard him talking about it. He said it's really some country to see. But it takes a lot of loot. I don't think I'll ever save enough money to go down that far. Always something to buy.

Start Early

This summer McKinney Construction is building HUD houses back at the new site. They got boys working there for twenty dollars an hour. My son is working there now. I talk to him everyday about his job.

I even have to go to bed early on account of him because I get him up every day. They work six days a week. He's just a teenager and he likes to ride around. But he don't drink yet. I told him, "Junior, if you're going to drink you can't stay under my roof. The first bottle you buy you got to think you can handle the booze. Well, I guess you can be on your own from there on." I told him that I don't know how many times. "That's the way your brother went." I told him that too but he thought I was just scolding him. I was saying that for his own good.

I tell my son now that he's working he has to get to work on time. I tell him, "That school is right next door to me but I leave the house ten minutes to eight every morning. Sometimes twenty minutes to eight. Don't take me five minutes to walk to school but you got to start early. Leave twenty minutes or fifteen minutes ahead of the job. Maybe your motorbike won't work and you have to run. At least you won't be late. This is the first job you're on. You got long years ahead of you to make yourself a living. You got to get used to that. How many years I been working at the school? I have to leave ten minutes to eight. I don't leave right at eight o'clock straight up and down all these years. Because you've got to take your time and make sure you got everything you need. You start rushing around, that's when you'll get hurt. You guys are doing heavy work back there. If you get there five minutes late you'll be nervous and the boss will think you're lazy.

"And don't mind about other guys. They've had jobs before and they know what they're doing. You, you're just starting. Be there ahead of time. The boss see you always before the hour, they think this guy likes to work. You've got to do that. If you're going to think of going to college, you've got to make your own money. You can't have it so easy." Well he's trying. But then I told him, "The minute I hear you take that drink and you buy the first bottle of booze, there is the door. If you think you can buy that booze and make a living for yourself, fine. You can put a roof over yourself. But not in my room."

This guy back here, the boss, started out hiring guys right and left for the beginning of work. He's testing them out. He hires some guys for three or four hours and then lays them off. Just keep checking them out like that. So I told my son when he first got hired don't fool around with another kid. If the kid is on just forget about him. Just like you don't know him. Don't start talking and playing because that boss is checking on you guys. He's going to start picking from the bottom up. That's the way he's doing. Now he's just got picked-out men.

Junior's been at it for awhile but I still talk to him every day. Every time he gets off work. Every morning. I keep talking to him. Just like he don't want it all right but he's got to take it. He's got to learn to make a living for himself. He figures to go to mechanic's school this fall so he'll try to stick it out.

Chapter Five: Drowning

Fish wheels at Nulato.

James' Last Fourth of July

We just dropped our net back in across from Nine Mile Bluff and the bushing went out on our prop. We barely made it back across. Simeon Mountain saw we were having trouble so he was waiting for us by the bluff. I had another prop in town so we came up with Simeon to get it. Just as we were landing my son James was packing gas down to his boat.

I told him no use to go down. We started up his wheel already. I knew he was drinking. Fourth of July, you know. There was another man with him. Both of them took off going down while I was mixing gas and taking the prop off my other kicker.

We went back down in our little boat with a twenty horse kicker. At Seven Mile, Bergman had a camp. He has his family there fishing. James waved at us from the bank as we went by.

Back down at the bluff the teachers, Brian and Theresa Zincke invited us for a cup of coffee. They just got there ahead of us. They don't fish commercial, only for their dogs. As I was changing the prop on the fifty I heard James' boat start up. We were waiting for the coffee and pretty soon here comes that guy from Manley, Steve O'Brien, in his boat. As soon as he see us he came right in. My wife said there's something wrong.

He landed and told us James went down. Oh, it hurt us. Right away we came up but we didn't know where he went in. Steve was at Four Mile and he was coming down to visit James. He thought he was on his wheel. But he said last time he saw water splash was little below the two wheels. It was windy, choppy. He got all upset. Well, when you see a guy in the water and you're that far away, you just get a little off your mind, I guess.

I know because I was there when my half-brother Harry Brush drowned near Two Mile Island. I was fishing for a living then at Six Mile. He came up pushing a rowboat with a one lunger inboard boat. He was coming up pretty slow so I waited for him at my camp and then tied my boat on and helped him. I didn't know they had homebrew and they were getting drunk.

This little twenty foot boat they were pushing was loaded down with fish. Fish dried and packed fifty in a bale. Harry was going out to check the little boat to see if it was leaking. There was a roll of heavy green tarp there. He kicked it and fell right overboard. His wife and his daughter, the one they adopt, was in the boat. I reached down with one arm but I just tipped him. So I jumped over to his boat, stop his motor and jump back to mine. By that time his wife got wild with me.

I start pulling the engine in reverse. I reverse for so far till I thought I was past him. Here he floated up about twenty feet below me. That roll of tarp was floating right alongside of him. He was belly up and moving his arms. Didn't even try to swim. I hollered, "Try to grab that canvas!" I even threw the pike pole in the water to him. Nothing.

I had to hold his wife and his kid he adopt and try to work his engine. The damn motor quit with me when I put in in reverse too fast. I killed the motor. We stopped. It used a rope to start. You have to wind the rope around it and pull the flywheel. And sometimes it didn't start right away. Finally when I start it and reverse, he was already down.

Franklin Madros was coming up with a ten horse Johnson outboard. He happened to be about mile and a half below us at the point of Devil's Island. Right there he ran out of gas. He had kind of a hard time filling up his tank and getting his kicker started again. He caught us up on the other side of the island. We were just coming in. I had chopped the line off that one boat and rammed it into the bank.

We came back and made grab hooks right away. We started searching. There was a water snag sticking up and I thought it was around there. He went down there alright but he had to drift before he hit bottom. It took us seven and a half hours before someone fished him out. The nurse was there, too. She said he hit the side of the boat and broke his nose. He was already knocked out when he hit the water.

When my boy drowned I stayed at camp twenty-four hours a day. Steve came down. Somebody always volunteer to stay the night with me. My brother was staying at the Nine Mile Bluff right where the current hits. We stayed there thirteen days. The thirteenth day they found him floating.

Leroy Sommers just came down from the slope. He and his dad went down to my brother at the bluff. Fishing was closed for the week. Freddie came back up to our camp to stay overnight. Andy Durney was there. We took turns staying up. Whenever we fall asleep we just sleep for a little while. I usually couldn't sleep.

But I don't know what made me sleep that night. Every time I hear any boats or somebody talking I'm just wide awake again. Happened same way with my brother Arthur. He said he fell asleep the same time. Leroy Sommers and Tony Semaken seen something floating down. They pretty near let it go, but Leroy said let's go check it. Tony jumped in the boat with him. Here it was James.

My brother said he was so asleep he didn't even hear the kicker start. He didn't hear them until somebody woke him up. Then the whole bunch of guys, Edward Sipary and them, came up. All those boats and I didn't wake up. Not till Andy Durney came in my mosquito bed net and said, "Hey, they found James." Must have been about four o'clock in the morning.

Thirteen rough days working twenty-four hours a

day. Watching. People search, drag, search, drag. Every day. Well, my brother said, the best bet we got now is just to wait. So we start doing that. Waiting for him to come up. Then we thought we'd lose him. He might not float high enough to see. Leroy Sommers just happened to be right there. He seen his elbow. Just like an elbow floating down way out. Well, the current shoots right out from that bluff. They were just lucky to found him.

Same kind of search happened when this boy drowned below Last Chance. Water was cold yet in June. Bunch of guys with him all drinking. His folks built a camp there just like we did. Lean out with black tarp and searched. Searching, searching. Nothing. Eddie and I went down to the bluff to check our king salmon net. Here was Vincent Yaska and this boy's brother that drowned going down to Kaltag. They said they were going to go all the way to Kaltag. Search all the way.

They stayed down there a little while and started back up again. Calm, early in the morning. Just when the sun started coming up they hit that bluff again. Sun just smacks that place everytime it start coming up. Current comes right along the shore. Nine Mile Bluff. Nothing can miss that place. Vincent told this boy, "We're going to wait here for awhile."

They went up on the hillside with binoculars. Water was kind of high but there was no drift. Pretty soon Vincent looked around and this other guy whose brother drowned was asleep. Vincent looked upriver in the binoculars and he seen something coming. Floating. He might have had a jacket or shirt on, I don't know. But he said he seen something waving like. Little breeze. You know how little breeze comes up once in awhile. He was kind of blowed up floating high.

He didn't want to scare this brother or anything. He woke him up easy and talked to him. Vincent said, "Don't get nervous or don't get excited if we happen to see anything." They got in the boat and headed straight for it. Sure enough it was that guy floating.

That's about twenty miles he floated. Well, they searched and searched.

His poor brother and mother and father had camp right there. They lean out with black tarp just like we did. That was their best bet to just wait.

For my son that was the best bet, too. I sure appreciate them guys that used to stay up with me. Fishing going on. Middle of commercial season. They have to work all day fishing and then they come back and stay with us. They keep searching and dragging. They drag the whole place and they drag it again. Trying, trying, trying. We didn't know where he floated up or nothing. Thirteenth day they found him. It was really hard. I don't know how many times a night I go up from my camp to the wheel. Walk forward and back. Walk forward and back, watching for something. We pulled in our wheels to give clearance. People thought he might be around there. Dragging, we fish out of the water everything we lost before. Piece of wire or piece of cable, but we never could fish out the body. Just floating we got him.

Under The Ice

Three or four years ago in the winter, Vernon Sommers went through an open hole in the ice right on the other side of Koyukuk Island. Snow machine and everything went down. There was three of them on two machines. The other two grabbed each other, drifted to the ice and jumped out. When we got there one girl's rabbit skin mitts was still frozen to the ice.

They chartered some divers up from Anchorage to dive for the body. They went down I don't know how many times. Silty river, muddy. Hard to see even with their underwater flashlights. But they tell us how the bottom is. That place has got a rut there, and another one over here. The snow machines down right here. One is a 250 the other one is 300.

The open hole was pretty big but the divers didn't want to get under the ice to search. I don't blame them, if the safety line goes they're goners, too. We cut the ice towards the beach for them. They said the current was about four feet down and then just dead water. No way the body will move. They

Nulato caches.

A Nulato home.

Old section of the graveyard overlooking Nulato.

say they can tie a line to the snow machines if we want to fish them out. But we don't care about the machines, we want the body first.

We searched and searched. It took us about four days. This was December. We went back up there again. The whole bunch, just about the whole village. We cut the ice into the beach with a chainsaw. Two feet thick already. We just kept chipping it off with chain saw. One boy from Koyukuk started dragging. Walking along upsteam dragging the hook. Fourth day he fished him out.

That was the first one right close by to the village that drowned through the ice around here. We hear some other places they drown but they get them out easy because it's either in a lake or dead water. Then they go right straight down. This was right in the current.

Try To Be Careful

Last couple of years the Camp Fire Girls have been teaching the little kids how to swim. That's really good for them to learn how to swim. Anything could happen. Now if they get by themselves, they'll know what to do. But a lot of drowning is caused by carelessness.

Careless driving like how I lost my son. I got all kind of life jackets there in the house. Hanging in the shed. He had a brand new life jacket he should leave in the boat all the time. You see it's just drinking, carelessness. Don't use a life jacket or anything. If all the people just be careful driving, this stuff would hardly happen.

Now people got high powered kickers on small boats. And they know they'll get to the liquor store in Last Chance. No matter how slow they go that booze or beer will never run away from them. That's what really hurts. But they just push that throttle right down far as it will go to get there fast. They don't care if they're hitting drifts or ice or anything. Plywood boats, heck, when you hit them underwater log, you might tear off the whole end of your boat. Then you got no place to go. Most of them got no life-jackets on and get drunk on the boat. They should wait till they get back on the beach and other people around. Sometimes they want to show off and make sharp turns.

James' wife is raising their kids. The oldest one is in grade two now. The second one is a girl, she's going to start grade one next fall. But the youngest one wouldn't even be in kindergarten next year. He was just about two or three weeks old when his father died.

Stickdance

This spring, March 7-13, 1983, at the Stickdance we dressed ten people for James. My wife started working making things the year after he drowned. She'd knit one afghan, maybe take a month. Then she knit socks and gloves. And if somebody is not doing anything, she'd hire them to knit, too. For three or four years she knit and sewed a lot of stuff. Every trip to Fairbanks she'd buy stuff on sale and just pile it up.

You talk to older people, it wasn't like that years ago. All that stuff had to be made out of fur. Not like now. You can open Eddie Bauer books and order parka. Used to be they sew maybe squirrel skin parky. Take long time. Those old people say now its easy. Not much money in the old

Dinnertime during Stickdance week in Nulato, 1983. Families putting on the Stickdance feed visitors and other residents of Nulato each night of the week-long celebration. Pauline Peters is in the center.

57

days. No jobs. Everything was done by trapping.

Now the Stickdance is over. We did it. We did what was right. I can sleep good now. You have to talk with my wife about what's behind the Stickdance. She was raised in it and knows all about it. I don't know much, but they say after somebody dies until you have Stickdance it's just like they're wandering around yet. Then they might get lonesome and take their friends with them. We have to do certain things so their spirit can rest. It's lot of work and take lot of money. Now it's over and we did the best we could.

Singing and dancing during the 1983 Nulato Stickdance.

1983 Nulato Sickdance singers and dancers.

58

People dancing around the Stickdance pole arm in arm. Their movement can be seen as a blur in the photo.

A closer view of some of the same people dancing around the pole in the above photo. L-R: (far left) Kevin Mountain, Gladys Ekada, Eleanor Laughlin, Miranda Wright, Edith Nicholas, Ida Hildebrande, Henry Ekada, Donna Sadowski.

People who have been dressed by families putting on the 1983 Nulato Stickdance. They have been dressed in new clothes from head to foot in honor of the deceased. L-R: Carl Noble, Fred Stickman Jr., George Peter, Harry Demoski, unidentified.

The Wash Tub dance, the final event of Stickdance week. As each person enters the Community Hall they dance in front of the tarp and singers. Some bring treats such as cookies, candies or cigarettes which are set on the tarp. The treats are distributed at the end of the dancing.

Yvonne Yarber

Gifts being given to Stickdance visitors by families of the deceased being honored. Elders and people who helped the families during their time of grief are given extra special gifts. L-R: Martha Joe, Sister Ann Evelyn, Mildred Stickman and Henry giving out fur. Nulato, 1983.

More Wash Tub dancers, 1983.

Photo by Glenn Olsen

Card playing at the 1983 Kaltag Stickdance and Carnival. Clockwise around the table: Curt Madison in the plaid shirt, unidentified, Henry Ekada, Henry Agnes, George Madros standing in the doorway, unidentified, Franklin Madros, Plasker Nickoli.

Nulato children playing, 1982. L-R: John Ekada, Todd Nickoli, Vernon Hildebrande, Allen McGinty, unidentified.

Henry Ekada, 1979.

Index